SEA PSALMS

Sea Psalms

John Jay Hughes

TWENTY-THIRD PUBLICATIONS
Mystic, Connecticut

For Gene
a generous shipmate
a faithful friend

Twenty-Third Publications
P.O. Box 180
Mystic CT 06355
(203) 536-2611

© 1988 John Jay Hughes. All rights reserved. No part of this publication may be duplicated without prior written permission of the publisher. Write to Permissions Editor.

ISBN 0-89622-361-2
Library of Congress Catalog Card Number 88-50446

Edited by John G. van Bemmel
Cover and book design by William Baker
(Photo credits on the last page of this book.)

CONTENTS

Introduction	6
"Launch Out into the Deep" (Luke 5:4)	13
At Dawn	15
For Perfectionists	17
In Discouragement	19
For Perseverance	21
On Setting Out	23
For Wisdom	25
Humility	27
"He Buried His Master's Money" (Matthew 25:18)	29
Mid-Passage	31
The Journey, Not the Destination	33
"Come Aside and Rest Awhile" (Mark 6:31)	35
A Psalm of Praise	37
Coming into Port	39
A New Day	41
For Shipmates	43
In Failure	45
Journey's End	47

INTRODUCTION

The plane that brought me across the Atlantic to John F. Kennedy Airport landed at three o'clock on a sunny winter afternoon, Thursday, January 18, 1984. It had been similarly sunny at takeoff from Schipol Airport in Holland seven-and-a-half hours earlier. As the plane climbed, I could see Amsterdam and the surrounding waterways spread out beneath me. I knew that watery labyrinth well from cruises with boys at the German school on the Dutch frontier where I was then teaching. There, two days previously, I had learned of my father's death in Newport, Rhode Island. Now I was coming home for his funeral.

By five o'clock I was flying east on a smaller plane over Long Island Sound. I recalled the family cruise down there in a chartered sailing yacht in June 1944. A month past my sixteenth birthday and just graduated from prep school, I was about to enter Harvard in early July. I considered myself very grown up. Starting college was far more important than sailing, especially with my family. I must have been a severe trial to them.

From the air, I followed the whole of the Connecticut

shore as it passed by to port. Then came Fishers Island and Block Island off to starboard as we turned north to fly up Narragansett Bay to Providence. The sun was just setting. All at once, I saw my whole childhood spread out beneath me like a carpet. It was a magical moment.

I knew every inch of those waters. There, as a little boy, I had learned from my father how to sail. There, in Newport Harbor, between Long Wharf and the Naval Torpedo Station, we were caught one day in a squall in our Newport Yacht Club dory, *Typhoon*. My mother was with us, so I cannot have been more than six, for she died when I was six and a half. We suffered a partial knockdown and water began to pour over the lee rail into the open boat. I screamed in terror, certain that our last hour had struck.

"Jay, be quiet," my father shouted at me indignantly. We did not capsize. We didn't even fill. My father's rebuke was justified and my fear had been unfounded. But I made an important discovery that day (though I would not realize it till years later). I was something my father often mentioned in tones of scornful contempt: a Fair Weather Sailor. I have never been able to pretend that I was enjoying myself when wet or terrified. At sea in my father's company I was frequently both. I developed an early antipathy to his cheerfulness in the midst of discomfort and wondered how he could be so different.

I have since been heartened to find that there are seamen far more accomplished than either of us who are also Fair Weather Sailors. "I prefer it calm," the world-renowned Captain Irving Johnson told me in the great cabin of his beautiful ketch *Yankee* in a harbor on the west coast of Sweden a quarter century ago. And referring to his numerous passages under sail around Cape Horn, he added: "You couldn't buy me to go there today." Now there's a man I warm to.

The Fair Weather Sailor par excellence, however, and a man truly after my own heart, is the British yachtsman who was my guest one evening in the harbor of Crookhaven at the southwest corner of Ireland aboard my little ketch, *Floodtide*. As we finished the second bottle of fine vintage wine (which I had laid down in the bilge for such special occasions) I told him of my frequent bouts with despondency when, overtaken by foul weather at sea, uncertain of my position, and too seasick to work it out from the rapidly disappearing data, I knew I had no business being out there, endangering my life and the lives of those foolhardy enough to put to sea under my command. At such moments, I confessed, I knew that the only decent and courageous thing to do was to put the boat up for sale as soon as I reached harbor.

How delighted I was to discover from my visitor's reply that I was not the cowardly weakling I had taken myself for when sailing with my father in childhood. "In bad weather at sea," he assured me, "all yachts are for sale."

Now as we flew north toward Providence, I could see the patch of water just south of little Rose Island where I had caught my first mackerel. I was sailing that day not with my father, but with a Norwegian-American named Lars Larsen, a mariner almost as ancient as his antique, gaff-rigged catboat. He had a lopsided face, something like a misshapen apple, and a glass eye. That was the reason, my father explained, why the eye did not move like the other one. Mr. Larsen's bizarre appearance, he told me, came from his having been blown up in Havana harbor in 1898 as a sailor aboard the battleship *Maine*. Lars Larsen had taught my father and his brothers to sail. My father thought it would be good if he took me out and showed me a thing or two. He did so in a manner very different from what I was accustomed to: calmly, quietly, with no shouting. I liked that.

Down there I could just make out the pier on Newport's Washington Street where I had watched the first boat of my very own being lowered into the water for her maiden voyage. What did it matter that she was only six feet long, flat-bottomed, straight sided, and equipped with only two thwarts to sit on, and a pair of oars? To me she was the most glorious craft in the world. My six-year-old breast fairly burst with excitement as I watched this vessel take the waves.

My father had given her to me (or told me he was doing so) the previous Christmas. I could hardly believe that anything so wonderful was to be mine. She was built by the same Lars Larsen in his backyard. One of the first things we did when we got to Newport that June was to go and inspect the boat under construction.

This little skiff was the source of endless hours of childhood fun, summer after summer. Within a few weeks I not only could row her proficiently, but had even mastered the art of sculling: propelling the boat forward by means of a single oar resting in a half-circle cut out for this purpose in the stern.

There below too I could make out Codrington Cove, where I came to grief because of overconfidence in this new skill. Foolishly I tried to tow the much larger *Typhoon* with the skiff, not by rowing with two oars (which I could have managed), but by sculling. The weight of the much larger vessel soon dragged us down to leeward, and my fate was sealed by my rashness in taking only one oar with me. In no time at all the prevailing southwest wind drove me in the skiff, and the *Typhoon*, against the causeway leading to the Naval Training Station and War College. My father, who had watched this deteriorating situation from an upstairs window ashore, came storming down to set things to rights, telling me never again to attempt anything so foolhardy.

In those same waters I could remember seeing the

magnificent J-boats that used to race for the America's Cup in the 1930s. How often I watched with fascination as these prodigious craft, more than 100 feet overall with a professional crew of 24, left their moorings and raised a flood of canvas. Even commercially sponsored syndicates cannot afford to build such vessels today. I shall always be grateful to have seen them.

In those waters, too, I often sailed round the enormous power yachts of the Super-Rich: Vincent Astor's *Nourmahal*, J.P.Morgan's *Corsair*, the *Aloha* of Arthur Curtis James, the *Hiesmero* (whose owner I have forgotten), the magnificent square-rigger *Flying Cloud*, belonging to Marion Davies. Even the brightly polished and smartly manned tenders which ferried the owners and guests back and forth from shore were larger than our little *Typhoon*. My father scorned all power vessels, however, and called them "Stink Pots." I never shared his contempt. Even at a very early age it was clear to me that the people aboard them would not get cold and wet even in the worst weather. That appealed to me strongly.

How often I had crewed for my father in races down there. Later, on the Sakonnet River just visible far off to the east, I had myself raced the "Sakonnet sloop" he bought when I was ten, occasionally beating her designer, John Alden.

As these childhood memories came flooding back, I thought with love and gratitude of my father, who had made it all possible. Two days later we would lay him to rest in his native soil in a plain wooden coffin with rope handles, reminders of the sea he loved— a love he bequeathed to his children. As I write these lines, my younger brother is preparing to round the Cape of Good Hope in the 42-foot sailing yacht that has taken him from New England through the Panama Canal across the Pacific to Australia and South Africa.

My own sailing has been far less ambitious. My only ocean crossing was a passage from Finland to Bermuda in 1978. But I have cruised in two yachts of my own, and in a wide variety of chartered vessels, on both sides of the Atlantic, from the tropics almost to the Arctic Circle, and as far afield as Turkey and British Columbia. My abilities as skipper and navigator would gain me at best a passing grade.
I do not count myself an expert sailor, only a survivor. For that, however, and for the enormous amount of pleasure I have had on the ocean wave, I am deeply grateful. Not too many years ago I tried to persuade a fellow sailor that the Lord does not deduct from our alloted span the time we spend sailing. Though a man of faith (he happens to be an archbishop), he did not seem convinced. I cherish the belief nonetheless.

The "Sea Psalms" that follow reflect my experiences afloat. I send them on their way with the closing lines of the classic "Cruise of the Nona" by Hilaire Belloc, by all accounts an even less expert sailor than I am:

> The sea has taken me to itself whenever I sought it and has given me relief from men. It has rendered remote the cares and the wastes of the land; for of all creatures that move and breathe upon the earth we of mankind are the fullest of sorrow. But the sea shall comfort us, and perpetually show us new things and assure us. It is the common sacrament of this world. May it be to others what it has been to me.

"LAUNCH OUT INTO THE DEEP"
(Luke 5:4)

What is it, Lord, that lures me forth?
Why start the engine, cast off the lines, hoist sail?
Why embark upon a sea of troubles,
    the unknown dangers of the deep,
    when I could have security ashore?
Does the destination beckon—
    the nearby cove, the magic isle, the distant continent?
But all these I could reach by other means:
    more swiftly, in greater comfort,
    and without the perils that threaten my small craft.
Is it yearning for command?
    Yet often I have found command a burden,
    and often you have shown me, Lord, the limits of command:
    Ship and crew I may control at times,
    wind and wave never.
Does adventure call?
    Yet often I find boredom, and sometimes abject fear.
What is it, then, that lures me forth?
To this question I found no answer until you showed me, Lord.
You beckon me, beyond the far horizon.
"Launch out into the deep," you said to Peter and his crew,
    weary from a night of fruitless toil.
"Leave the still waters near the shore,
    abandon what you know and all security,
    and you shall find the great reward."
Help me, Lord, like them to venture and to dare,
    to do great things, for you.

AT DAWN

Thank you for this day, Lord, for the beauty of this place.
Thank you for bringing us here last night
    through the storm that pressed our little ship so hard,
    and the darkness that frightened us.
The rocks look so peaceful now.
Last night they were covered with angry waves
    and thrashing foam.
You kept us safe, Lord, amid every danger.
 I dedicate this day to you in thanksgiving.

Help me to be cheerful if it blows up again
    and we get cold and wet;
        to be patient when my friend drops something overboard
        (as I did yesterday),
        lets go the jib sheet, or loses the halyard up the mast
        (how often I've done that myself).
When I get tense and shout, remind me to say:
    "I'm sorry—it didn't mean anything."
 Help me to do the hardest jobs myself,
    to thank my friend for the fine meals he cooks,
    and for being so much more patient with me
    than I will ever be with him.

I dedicate this day to you, Lord,
    in thanksgiving.

FOR PERFECTIONISTS

Fair lines, perfect symmetry, exact workmanship—
    even in the hidden details no one would ever see.
That's the kind of work you did, Lord,
    in the carpenter's shop with Joseph.
They call them the "hidden years,"
    because they left no record.
They're wrong.
Your customers always got the best.
You understood their needs better than they did.
You used the best materials, you always met your deadlines,
    even when you were tired and had to work late.

Help me to be like that, Lord:
    to treat everyone with courtesy,
    to show patience, to be kind.
Help me when I'm tired and discouraged
    still to give my best;
    to strive for perfection
    yet not to fret when I fail to achieve it,
    because I'm human, not divine.
Help me to accept my humanity, my imperfection.

IN DISCOURAGEMENT

Can't find the buoy, Lord, and it's growing late.
If we don't find it, we won't know when it's safe to turn.
It's not lit either.
Don't keep us out here all night.
We found the first buoy, where the shallows begin.
The light was better then.
That was three miles back...or was it five?
If I'd written down the time
I could estimate the distance run.
I was overconfident.
They say the sea doesn't forgive.
But you do, Lord.
Forgive me now...forgive my carelessness and folly.
You promised to fetch home the lost sheep.
We're lost now...I think.
Fetch us home, Lord.
Bring our ship safe into port.

FOR PERSEVERANCE

"Too slow" you say? And I admit,
I sometimes think the same myself.
Five knots—or six or seven when the going's good—
    is no great speed.
But what's the use of double digits and a planing hull
    when you must shout above the roar,
    and throttle back in any kind of sea?
Afloat, ashore, we journey
    by perseverance, not by speed.
From far-off childhood I recall the tale
    of how the tortoise raced the hare
    and won because he never quit.
The snail too reached the ark by perseverance.
So with five knots I'll be content
    and grateful to the One who shapes my course,
And whom I hope to meet
    at journey's end.

ON SETTING OUT

Be with me, Lord, at the beginning of this day.
I cannot know what lies ahead.
Wind and weather are in your hands, not ours.
Take our little ship under your powerful protection.
Send your angels to guide and guard us on our course.
If the wind blows fair and the sun shines,
    fill our hearts with thankfulness.
If we encounter contrary wind and storm,
    give us courage and cool heads.
When we're too busy to think of you,
    don't you forget us.
I place our ship and crew in your hands, Lord.
And your hands are good hands.

FOR WISDOM

Thank you, Lord, for making me pull down that reef.
And thank you too for shipmates
    who work so fast and well.
With less canvas we're sailing better and faster.
Life is like that.
Attempt too much and you accomplish less.
Run too fast and soon you cannot walk.
Are we still pressing her too hard, Lord?
The wind has freshened since we reefed.
Don't like that big jib dipping in the drink.
Changing headsails in this wind will be hard work, though.
Don't want to send the crew forward if it's not necessary.
Should I douse the mizzen?...or the main?
So many doubts, decisions...in sailing, as in life.
Give me wisdom, Lord.
Show me what to do.
Help me do it.

HUMILITY

Our ship is so small, Lord,
    And your ocean is so large.
    That puts things in perspective.

I used to think humility
    was stooping to become small.
You've helped me see it's standing tall
    and measuring ourselves by your greatness.

The land has vanished; we're alone now.
How insignificant we seem, Lord,
    upon the vastness of your ocean.

I've heard it said you love each one of us
    as if in all creation there were only one to love.
Help me to be a prism of that love
    for sisters, brothers, who but for me
Might never glimpse the splendor of your love,
    vast, powerful, and deep as this sea on which we sail.

Enfold, embrace me, bear me up, Lord,
    immerse me in the ocean of your love.

"HE BURIED HIS MASTER'S MONEY"
(Matthew 25:18)

He thought he was being prudent.
In reality, he was cowardly.
He concentrated on security—and lost all.
If I were like him, Lord, I'd never leave harbor.

Out there, beyond the sheltering land,
    I find discomfort and uncertainty.
These are the price I pay
    for adventure, freedom, and romance—
For the sense of satisfaction that awaits
    when danger's past, the voyage ends,
And I can watch the anchor fall,
    make up the lines and go below,
To raise my glass and taste with friends
    the joy that only those can know
Who banish fear and heed your call.

You help us, Lord, to steer a course
    that we must plot afresh each day,
Until at last the voyage ends
    and you are there to say, "Well done."

MID-PASSAGE

How like to life is the voyage of a ship:
    the hopes and uncertainties on setting out;
    the overcoming of difficulties, only to find more;
    the solving of problems, only to meet greater.
Somewhere something always needs repair.
The daily, hourly tasks, are never done:
    navigation, maintenance of ship and gear,
    cooking, washing up, standing watch,
    keeping the log, sleep and (all too soon)
    the call to go on deck again.
We know times of deep joy:
    sunrise, sunset, good food and drink, shipmates' laughter;
And moments of awful fright:
    storm, fog, the dread sound of nearby ships we cannot see.
Most of the voyage, though,
    is somewhere between joy and dread,
Sometimes pleasant, often dull,
    making headway as best we can,
    in fair weather and in foul.
Progress seems so slow—
    until we look back and see how far we've come.

Stay with me, Lord,
    be my remaining voyage long or short.
Stay with me, guide my vessel safely into port.

THE JOURNEY, NOT THE DESTINATION

From deadlines, telephones, and meetings
    Good Lord, deliver me.
From time's tyranny, interruptions, and demands
    Good Lord, deliver me.
From letters, importuning pleas, and bores
    Good Lord, deliver me.

How sweet to shuffle off those chains,
    To raise the anchor, hoist the sail,
 And set a course—for where?
    It doesn't really matter where,
Or when I get there, or if I never do.

The journey's more important than the destination,
    Life's worth more than any end it serves.
 A voyage without set goal may be best of all,
    Freed from ambition's deadly thrall.

Today I'll leave the helm to you, Lord,
    While I sing "Alleluia," and "Glory be."
Failures past and cares to come I'll leave ashore
    Grateful for ship and sea, grateful for you.

"COME ASIDE AND REST AWHILE"
(Mark 6:31)

Think I'll just stay here, Lord,
    away from the machines and noise:
    cars, telephones, and planes—
Out of reach of others' voices,
    with their complaints and clamorous demands.
I know, the conversation of our shipmates
    is meant to help, cheer us, and encourage.
But you speak most often in silence.
Today I feel the need to go deep down
    into your recreating silence
    into the inner world of contemplation
    where I can be still and know
        that you are God.
So for today I'll leave the anchor down
    and turn loneliness into solitude,
    which is the loveliness of knowing
        that I'm alone with you.

A PSALM OF PRAISE

O you gannets and gulls, bless the Lord.
    Praise and magnify him forever.
O you sharp-eyed pelicans, bless the Lord.
    Praise and magnify him forever.
Swift schools of mackerel, bless the Lord.
    Praise and magnify him forever.
Frolicsome dolphins and seals, bless the Lord.
    Praise and magnify him forever.
All sea turtles and whales, bless the Lord.
    Praise and magnify him forever.
Let sand, seaweed, and rocks bless the Lord.
    Praise and magnify him forever.
You coral reefs and moray eels, bless the Lord.
    Praise and magnify him forever.
Clams, mussels, and oysters, bless the Lord.
    Praise and magnify him forever.
You crabs, lobsters, and scallops, bless the Lord.
    Praise and magnify him forever.
O calms, zephyrs, and gales, bless the Lord.
    Praise and magnify him forever.
In fog, sunshine, and rain bless the Lord.
    Praise and magnify him forever.
You snorklers, wind surfers, and divers, bless the Lord.
    Praise and magnify him forever.
Young men and maidens, old men, and children,
    bless the Lord.
    Praise and magnify him forever.
Let earth, sea, and air bless the Lord.
  For from him all things come, to him all return,
    who gives life to all and whom I will praise
        now and forever.
          Amen.

COMING INTO PORT

Didn't think we'd make it, Lord.
But here we are.
Battered, bruised, confused—but safe at last.
I thought it would be so easy.
Four hours, six at most, would see us safely into port.
That was before the fog came in,
and my navigation went out.
On such a beautiful day
There seemed no point bothering with those fussy details:
    compass course,
    time and distance run,
    position by cross bearings.
Then the fog closed in and I realized
    I'd been overconfident.
Too late I remembered:
    "Pride goes before a fall
    and vain heart before disaster."
Thank you, Lord, for keeping us from disaster.
Thank you for another lesson, another dose of your wisdom.
    "It is good for me that I have been in trouble.
    that I may learn your law."
Help me to remember that, Lord:
    to live by your wisdom, not my own;
    not to think I can cut corners with impunity.
Keep my ship on course—the course to you.

A NEW DAY

The wind howls above with awful whine.
    A halyard slaps against the mast.
I lie awake, thankful and afraid.
Thankful we're anchored, snug and safe;
    yet fearful from imagining
How we'd have fared outside
    had we not reached the cove in time.
What is it like out there right now?
If on the three-day passage still ahead
    we meet conditions such as these,
Shall we be equal to the test?
Our ship's so small, we're only three;
    fatigue, discouragement, and (worst of all) seasickness,
    have vanquished stronger crews than we.
Luck was on our side today
    (or was it you, Lord? I thank you anyway).
But who's to say we'll always be so fortunate?
Is the whole enterprise another case
    of my presumption, foolishness, and pride?

I feel the warm sun on my face
    I hear the gulls' cries overhead.
Whatever happened to the wind? It's gone.
    The crew's asleep. I'll try my best
To let them slumber on until
    the smell of coffee makes them stir,
And fill the cabin once again
    with their laughter, banter, cheer.

I thank you, Master of wind and sea,
    for this new day, for ship and crew.
Stay with us, guide us, keep us three
    happy with one another, grateful to you.

FOR SHIPMATES

They're all asleep now, Lord,
    and no wonder, after the day we've had,
battling against wind and tide;
    no wind at first, and then too much.

John and Diana, sharing a single bunk,
    three years married and still in love;
pressed close together, limbs intertwining;
    if they're not parents soon, it won't be for want of trying.

And then there's Paul, our master chef; and master too
    of the sardonic comment, of jests and quips.
I've never seen him down, or even blue.
    Who cares about his ignorance of ships?

Our first mate, Tom, came late to sailing.
    Most everything he knows of boats and navigation
he learned from me. He's steadier than I am though,
    companion on many cruises, treasured friend.

Was ever skipper so fortunate as I
    with shipmates so loyal, capable, and true?
I ask you, Lord, to bless each one.
    Bless our ship; keep us a happy crew.

IN FAILURE

Aground—and on an ebb tide too.
She won't float off till dark, that's sure.
Till then we've done the best we can.
The anchor's out at full scope
to pull her free when once we float.

Three weeks we've cruised on foreign shores
without mishap: no groundings,
navigation perfect every day.
And now this, so near our goal,
with the home harbor only hours away.

Why is it we so often come to grief
in waters we know best—when things go well, not ill?
To those whom we love most we show a side
we keep concealed from mere acquaintances:
childishness, self-centeredness, and pride.

I dare not thank you only for success, Lord.
From humiliation, failure I've learned more.
It's when I'm down and beaten I discern
your tender, loving mercy, and forgiveness;
the wisdom, strength, and peace for which I yearn.

JOURNEY'S END

The cruise is finished and the season too.
Cold winds, short days, herald the approach
of autumn. Already swimming's unappealing.
The few remaining surfers wear wetsuits.

The little ship that's given us such pleasure
is empty now, crew dispersed and gear ashore.
Topsides and brightwork are dull and faded,
evidence of hard use—but oh, what fun we had!

Tomorrow she'll be hauled.
A wooden cradle, not the waves, will be her bed
for the long winter sleep,
covered by lath and canvas against snow and ice.

Next spring we'll wake her, take the cover off,
clean sides and bottom, paint and varnish,
overhaul the engine—she'll need injectors,
and probably fresh batteries as well.

Will I be here to take the helm,
to steer her down the bay and out to sea
to new horizons, fresh adventures,
 as I've done so many times before?

Time, seasons, tide, and life itself
are in your hands, Lord, not ours.
So when you call I want you at the helm, Lord,
as pilot on my final voyage, the passage home, to you.

PHOTO CREDITS

Carol Freese Comeau: pages 12, 14, 16, 22, 34
Cyrus Richardson: page 18
J.H. Peterson: pages 30, 46
Photo-Boat/Ted Kelly: front and back covers, and pages 20, 24, 28, 32, 36, 44
Rhode Island Department of Economic Development: pages 26, 38, 40, 42
Drawing by Rembrandt Harmensz van Rijn (British Museum, London): page 6